This book belongs to:

_____

Leap into Life

Birthdays

January | February | March

April | May | June

July | August | September

October | November | December

Weekly Planner - Dates:

Monday

Tuesday

Wednesday

Thursday

Friday

Saturday

Sunday

To do
-
-
-
-
-
-
-
-
-
-
-

Notes

Notes, thoughts, ideas.

Weekly Planner-   Dates:

Monday

Tuesday

Wednesday

Thursday

Friday

Saturday

Sunday

To do

Notes

Notes, thoughts, ideas.

Weekly Planner-   Dates:

Monday

Tuesday

Wednesday

Thursday

Friday

Saturday

Sunday

To do

Notes

Notes, thoughts, ideas.

Weekly Planner- Dates:

Monday

Tuesday

Wednesday

Thursday

Friday

Saturday

Sunday

To do

Notes

Notes, thoughts, ideas.

Weekly Planner- Dates:

Monday

Tuesday

Wednesday

Thursday

Friday

Saturday

Sunday

To do

Notes

Notes, thoughts, ideas.

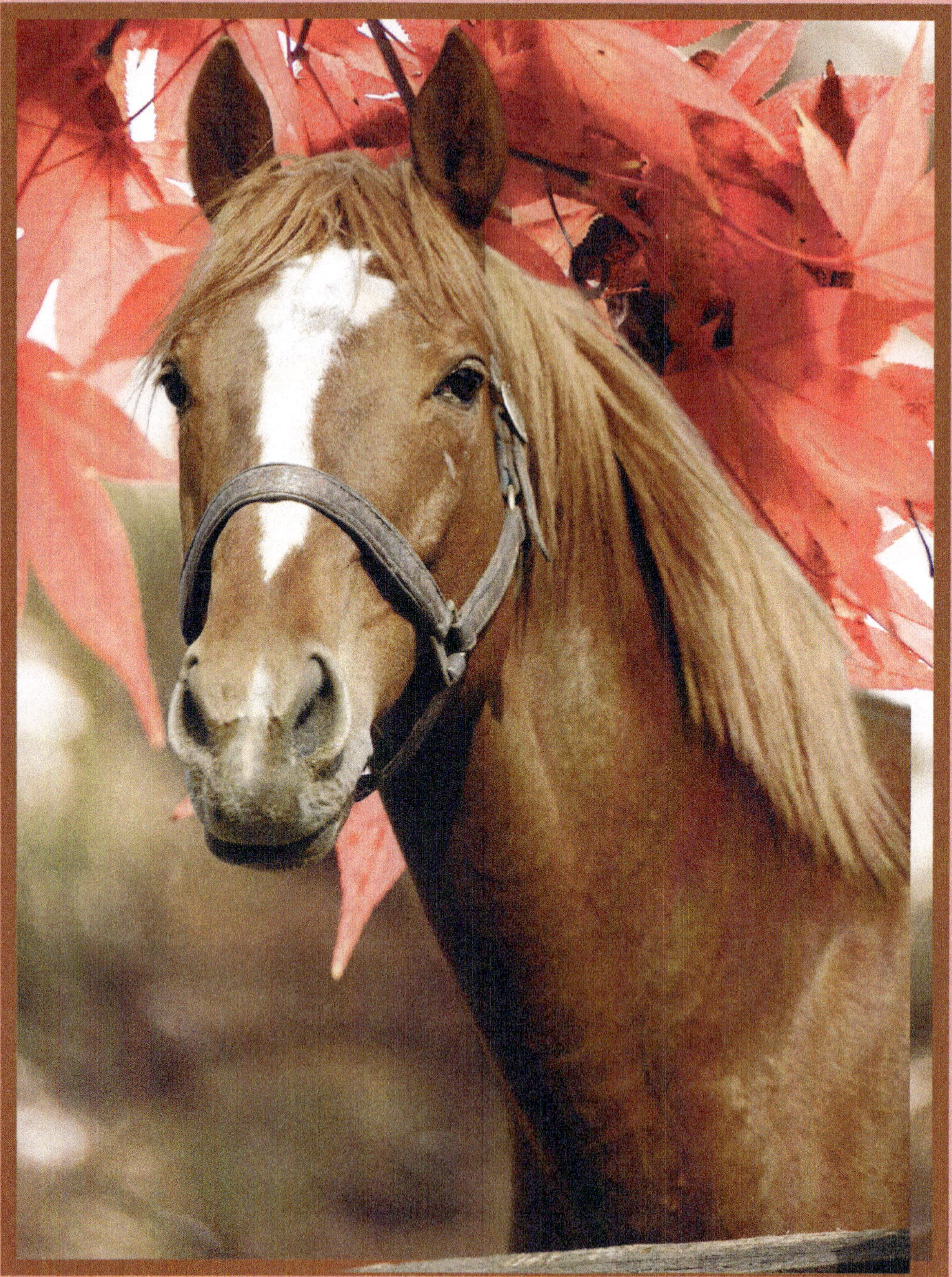

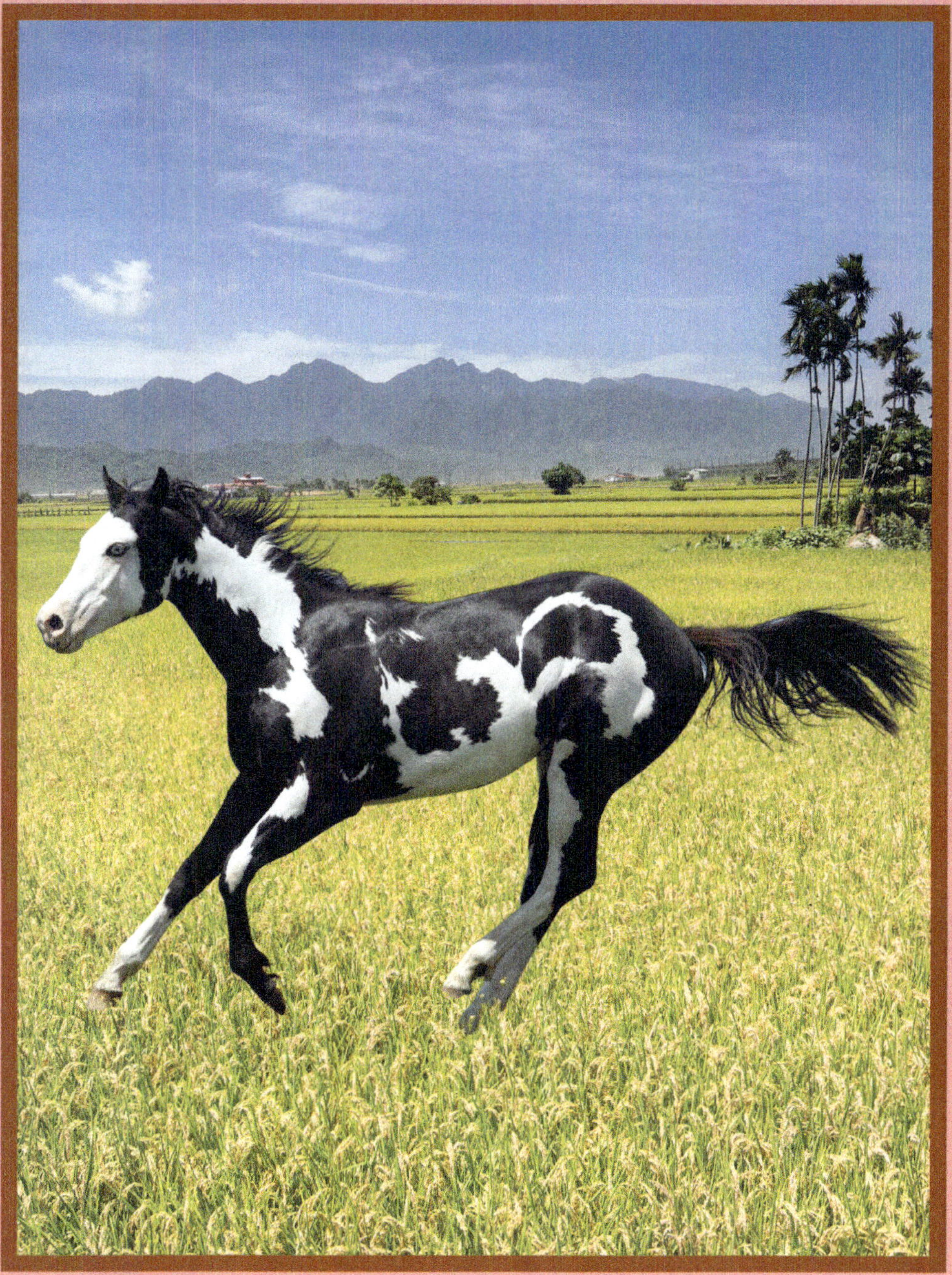

Weekly Planner- Dates:

Monday

Tuesday

Wednesday

Thursday

Friday

Saturday

Sunday

To do

Notes

Notes, thoughts, ideas.

Weekly Planner- Dates:

Monday

Tuesday

Wednesday

Thursday

Friday

Saturday

Sunday

To do
-
-
-
-
-
-
-
-
-
-
-

Notes

Notes, thoughts, ideas.

Weekly Planner-   Dates:

Monday

Tuesday

Wednesday

Thursday

Friday

Saturday

Sunday

To do
-
-
-
-
-
-
-
-
-
-
-

Notes

Notes, thoughts, ideas.

Weekly Planner- Dates:

Monday

Tuesday

Wednesday

Thursday

Friday

Saturday

Sunday

To do

Notes

Notes, thoughts, ideas.

Weekly Planner- Dates:

Monday

Tuesday

Wednesday

Thursday

Friday

Saturday

Sunday

To do

Notes

Notes, thoughts, ideas.

Weekly Planner-   Dates:

Monday

Tuesday

Wednesday

Thursday

Friday

Saturday

Sunday

To do

Notes

Notes, thoughts, ideas.

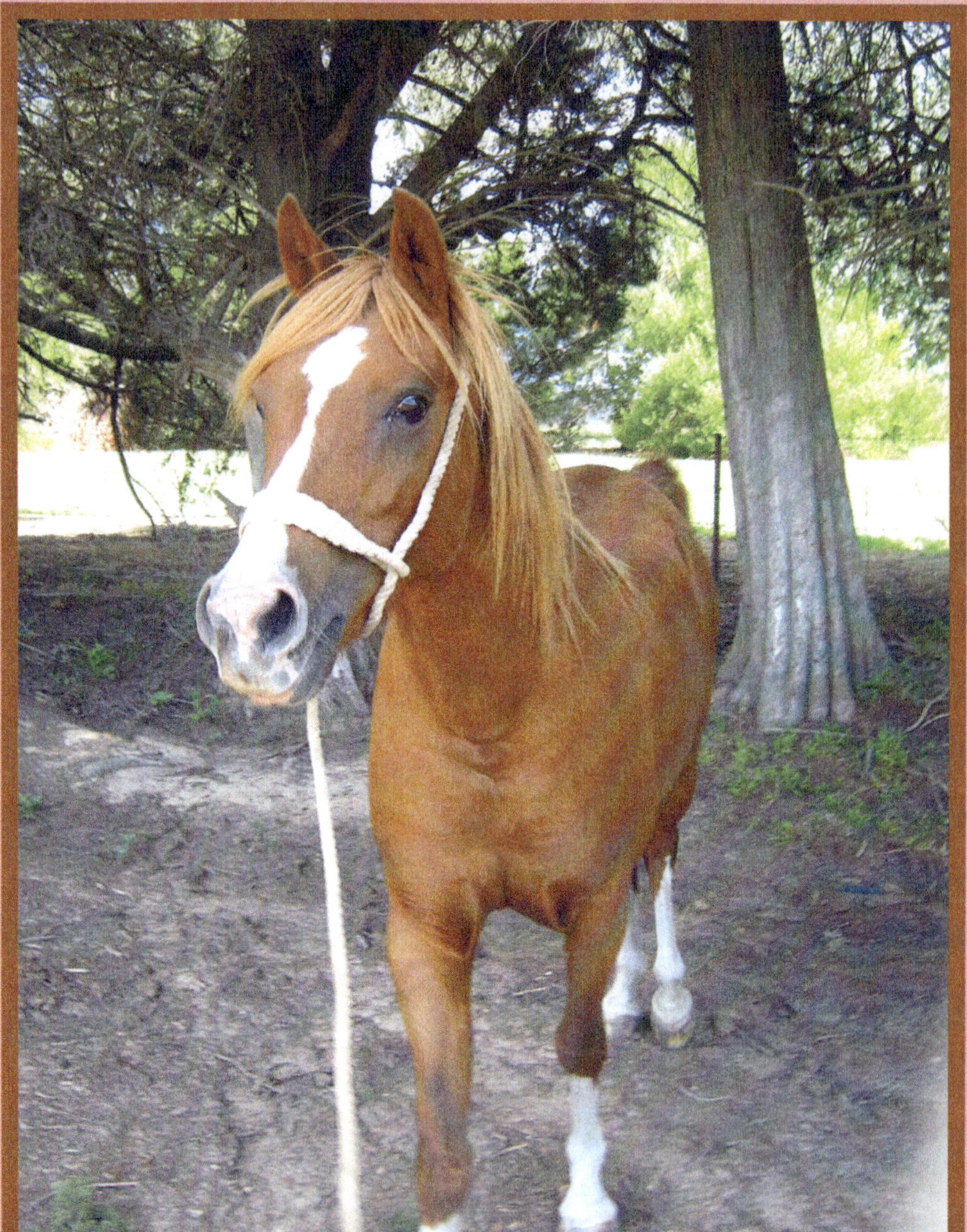

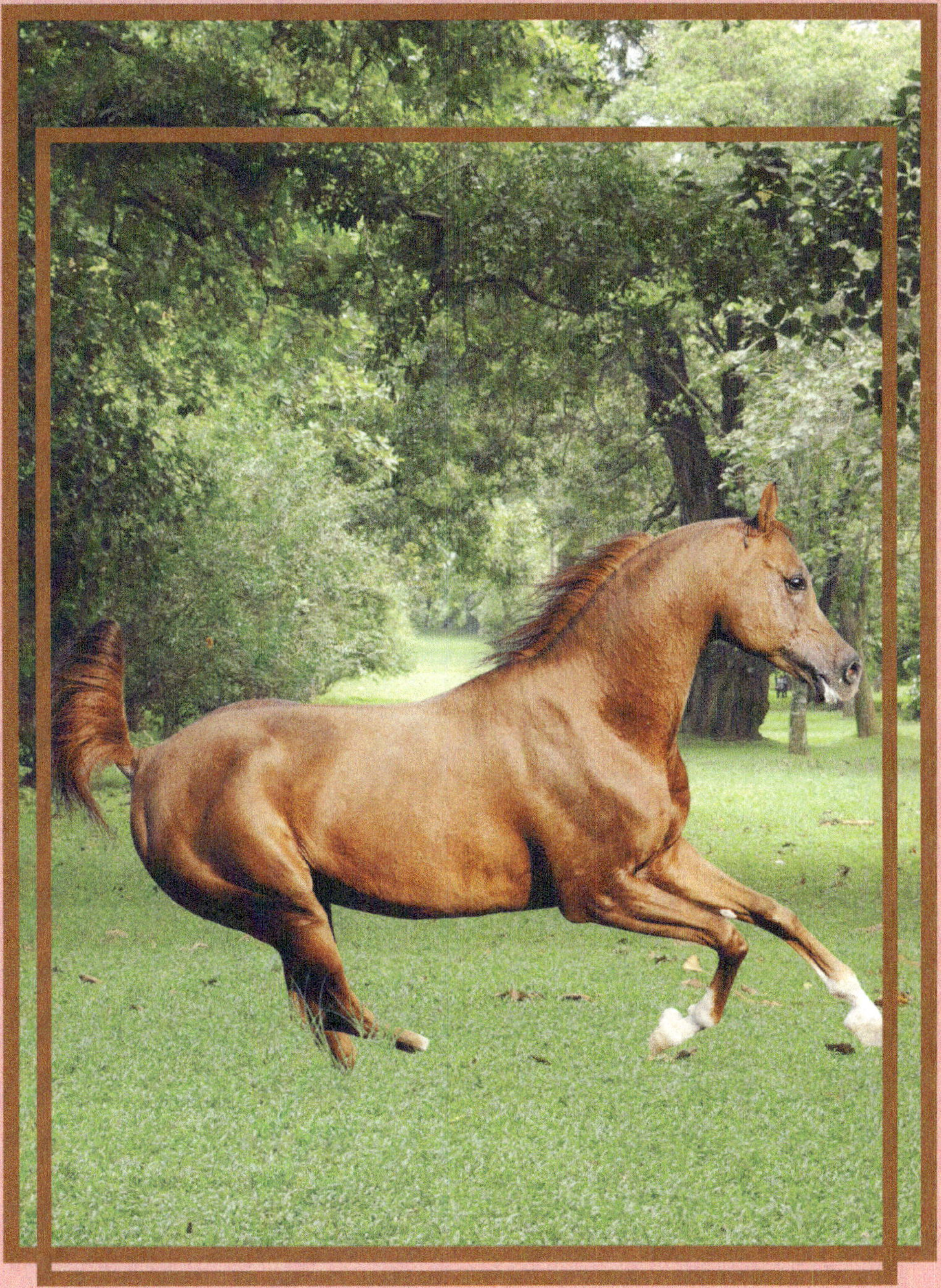

Weekly Planner- Dates:

Monday

Tuesday

Wednesday

Thursday

Friday

Saturday

Sunday

To do

Notes

Notes, thoughts, ideas.

Weekly Planner-   Dates:

Monday

Tuesday

Wednesday

Thursday

Friday

Saturday

Sunday

To do
-
-
-
-
-
-
-
-
-
-
-

Notes

Notes, thoughts, ideas.

Weekly Planner- Dates:

Monday

Tuesday

Wednesday

Thursday

Friday

Saturday

Sunday

To do
-
-
-
-
-
-
-
-
-
-
-

Notes

Notes, thoughts, ideas.

Weekly Planner- Dates:

Monday

Tuesday

Wednesday

Thursday

Friday

Saturday

Sunday

To do

Notes

Notes, thoughts, ideas.

Weekly Planner-   Dates:

Monday

Tuesday

Wednesday

Thursday

Friday

Saturday

Sunday

To do

-
-
-
-
-
-
-
-
-
-
-

Notes

Notes, thoughts, ideas.

Weekly Planner-   Dates:

Monday

Tuesday

Wednesday

Thursday

Friday

Saturday

Sunday

To do

Notes

Notes, thoughts, ideas.

Weekly Planner- Dates:

Monday

Tuesday

Wednesday

Thursday

Friday

Saturday

Sunday

To do

Notes

Notes, thoughts, ideas.

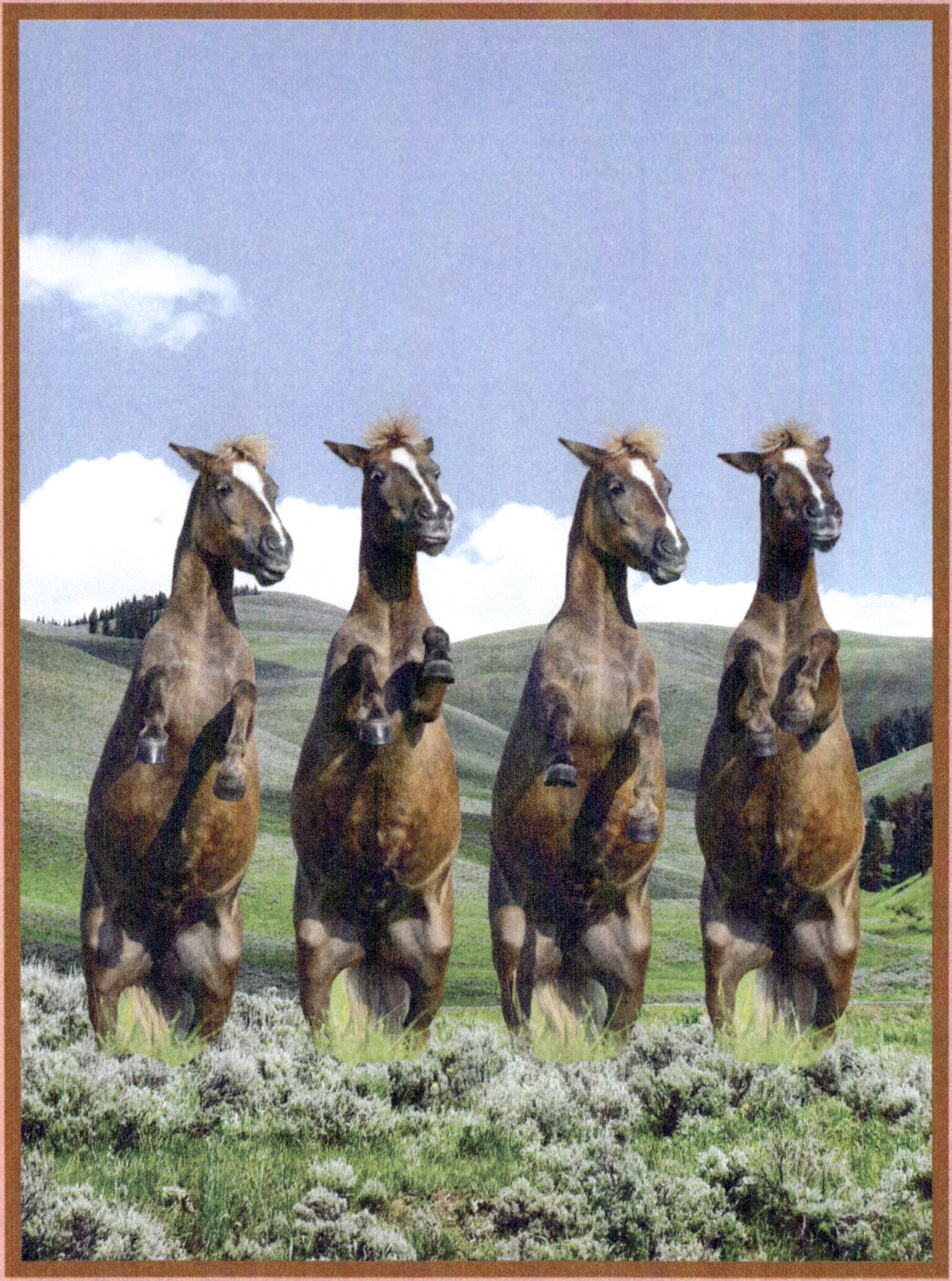

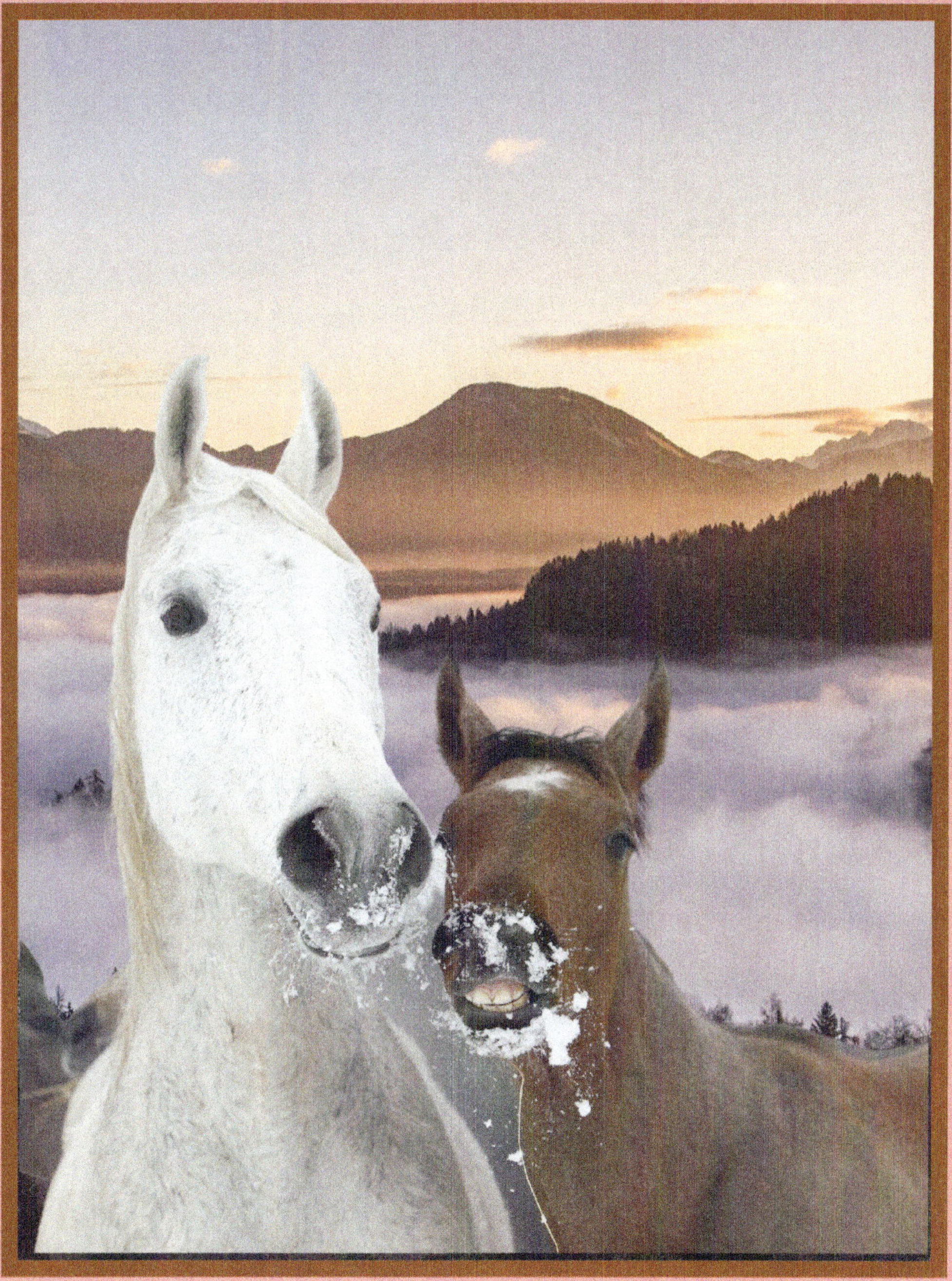

Weekly Planner- Dates:

Monday

Tuesday

Wednesday

Thursday

Friday

Saturday

Sunday

To do

-
-
-
-
-
-
-
-
-
-

Notes

Notes, thoughts, ideas.

Weekly Planner- Dates:

Monday

Tuesday

Wednesday

Thursday

Friday

Saturday

Sunday

To do

-
-
-
-
-
-
-
-
-
-
-

Notes

Notes, thoughts, ideas.

Weekly Planner-   Dates:

Monday

Tuesday

Wednesday

Thursday

Friday

Saturday

Sunday

To do
-
-
-
-
-
-
-
-
-
-

Notes

Notes, thoughts, ideas.

Weekly Planner- Dates:

Monday

Tuesday

Wednesday

Thursday

Friday

Satuday

Sunday

To do

Notes

Notes, thoughts, ideas.

Weekly Planner- Dates:

Monday

Tuesday

Wednesday

Thursday

Friday

Saturday

Sunday

To do

-
-
-
-
-
-
-
-
-
-
-

Notes

Notes, thoughts, ideas.

Weekly Planner- Dates:

Monday

Tuesday

Wednesday

Thursday

Friday

Saturday

Sunday

To do

-
-
-
-
-
-
-
-
-
-
-

Notes

Notes, thoughts, ideas.

Weekly Planner- Dates:

Monday

Tuesday

Wednesday

Thursday

Friday

Saturday

Sunday

To do

Notes

Notes, thoughts, ideas.

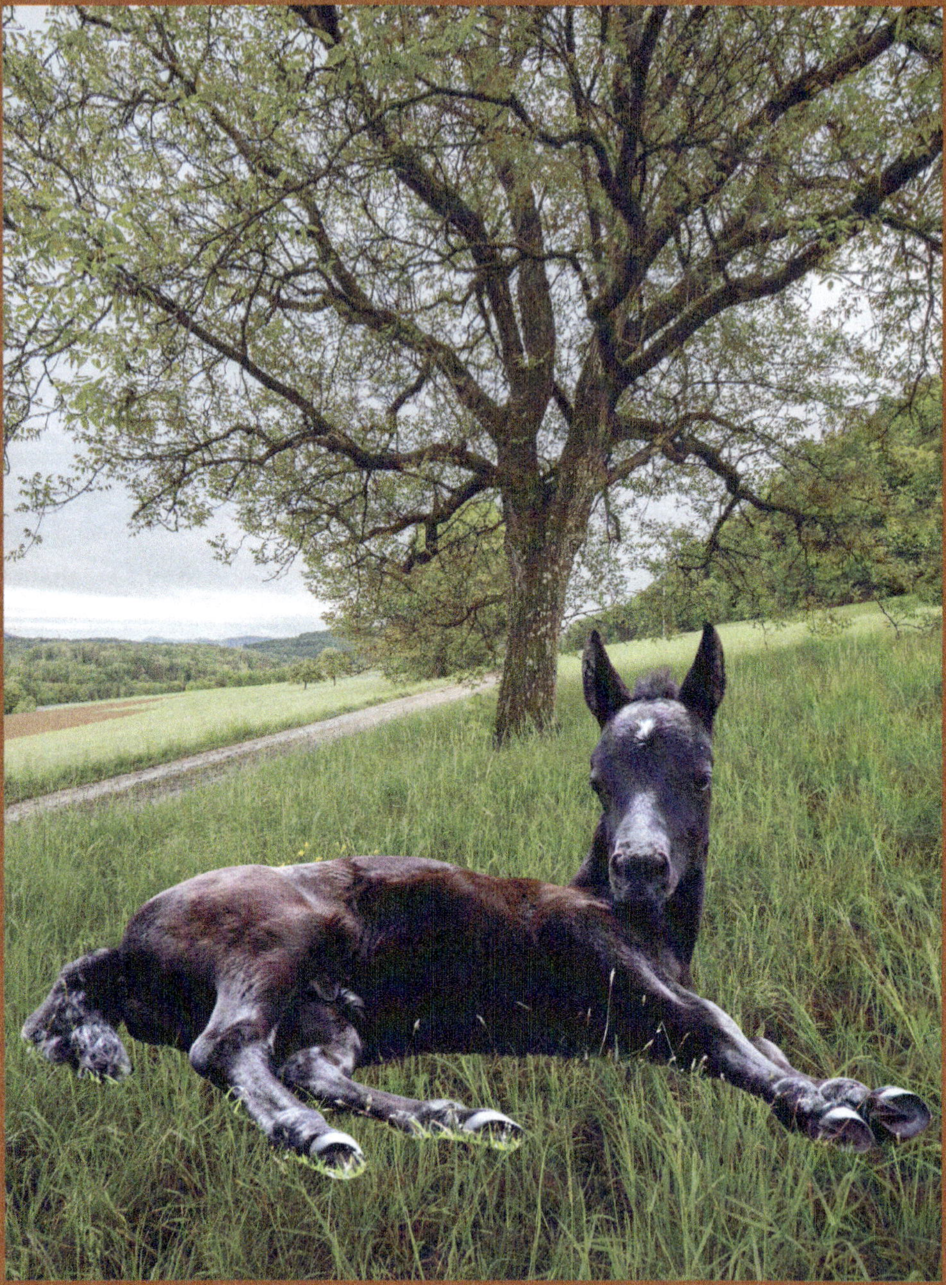

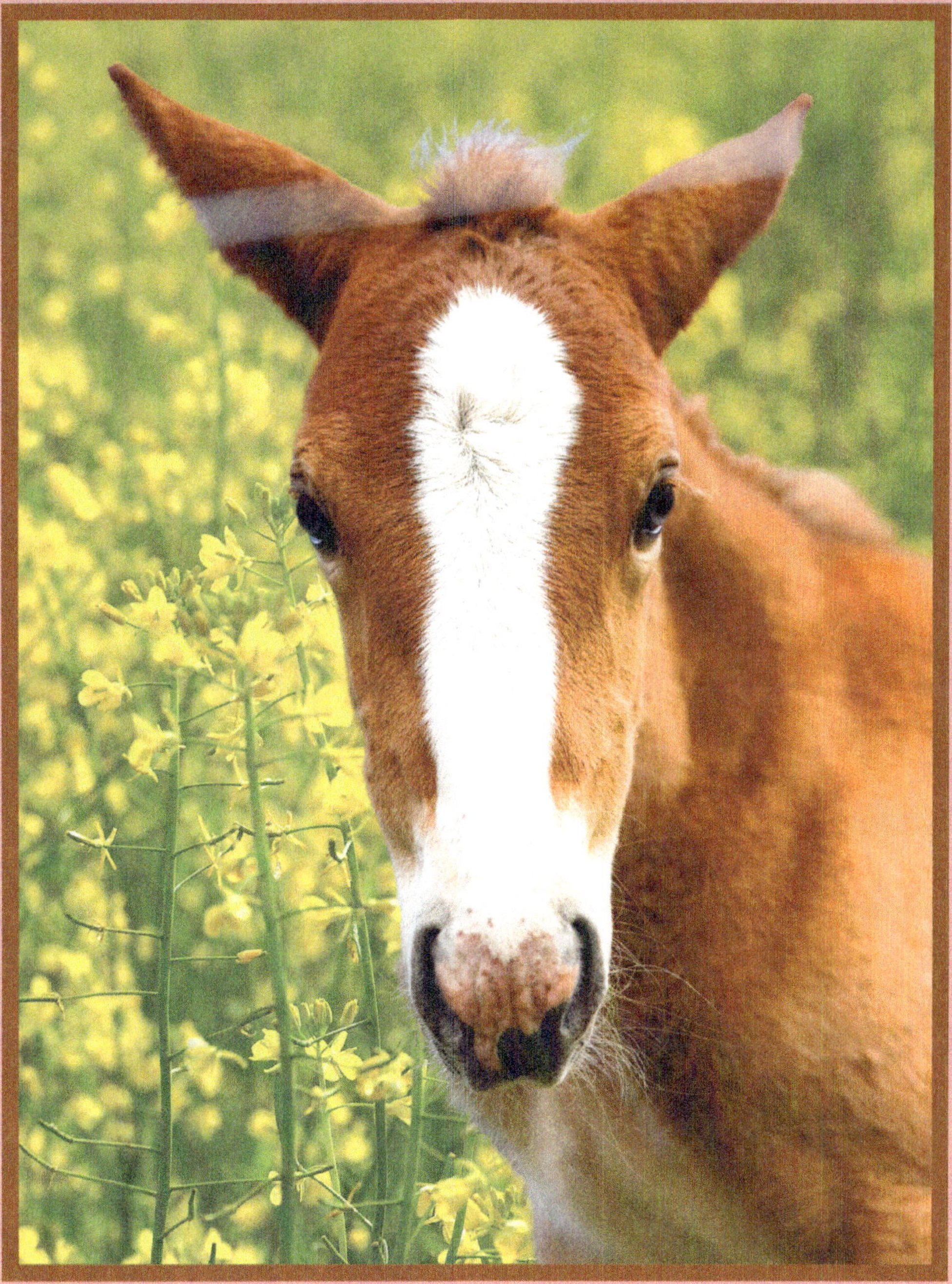

Weekly Planner- Dates:

Monday

Tuesday

Wednesday

Thursday

Friday

Saturday

Sunday

To do

Notes

Notes, thoughts, ideas.

Weekly Planner-   Dates:

Monday

Tuesday

Wednesday

Thursday

Friday

Saturday

Sunday

To do

Notes

Notes, thoughts, ideas.

Weekly Planner- Dates:

Monday

Tuesday

Wednesday

Thursday

Friday

Saturday

Sunday

To do

Notes

Notes, thoughts, ideas.

Weekly Planner-   Dates:

Monday

Tuesday

Wednesday

Thursday

Friday

Saturday

Sunday

To do

Notes

Notes, thoughts, ideas.

Weekly Planner- Dates:

Monday

Tuesday

Wednesday

Thursday

Friday

Saturday

Sunday

To do

Notes

Notes, thoughts, ideas.

Weekly Planner- Dates:

Monday

Tuesday

Wednesday

Thursday

Friday

Saturday

Sunday

To do
-
-
-
-
-
-
-
-
-
-
-

Notes

Notes, thoughts, ideas.

Weekly Planner- Dates:

Monday

Tuesday

Wednesday

Thursday

Friday

Saturday

Sunday

To do

Notes

Notes, thoughts, ideas.

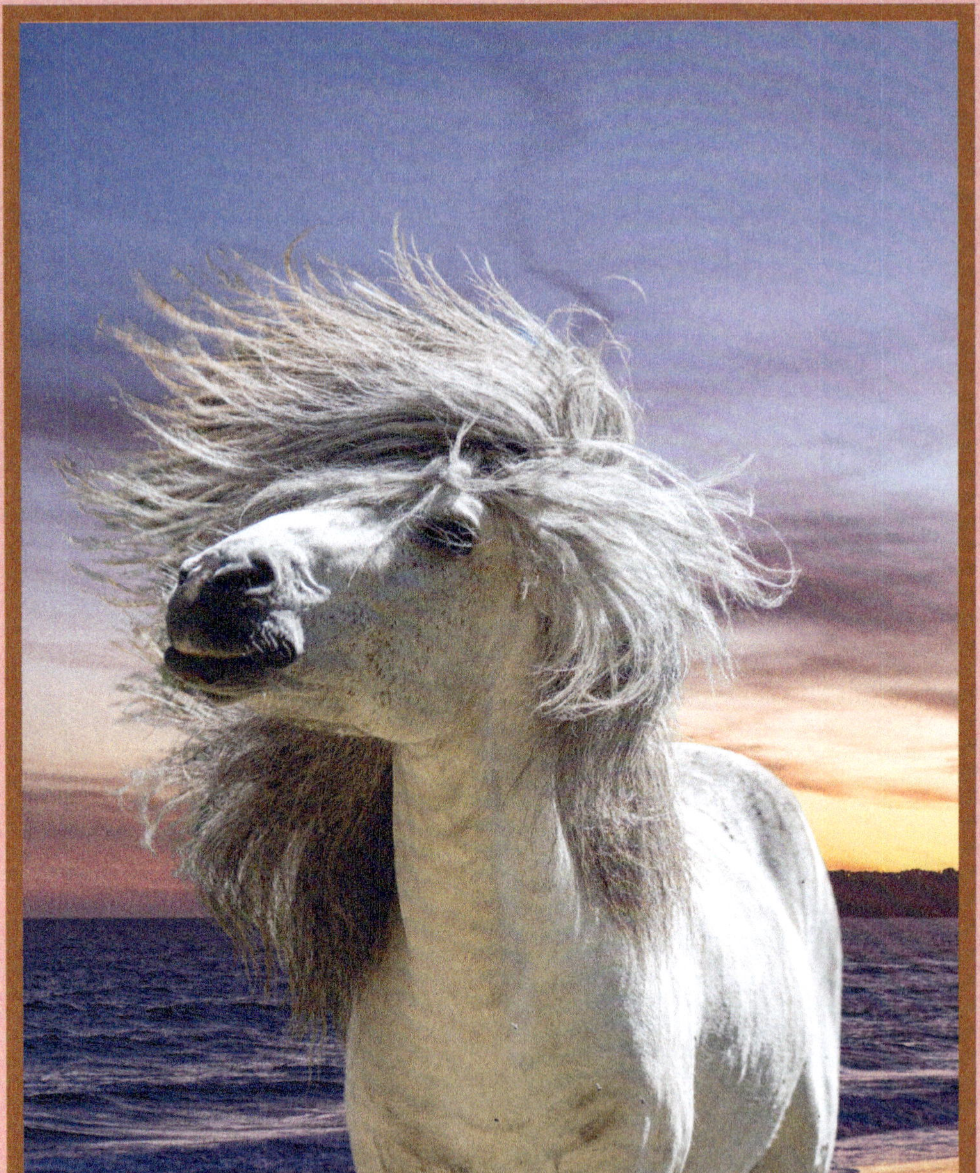

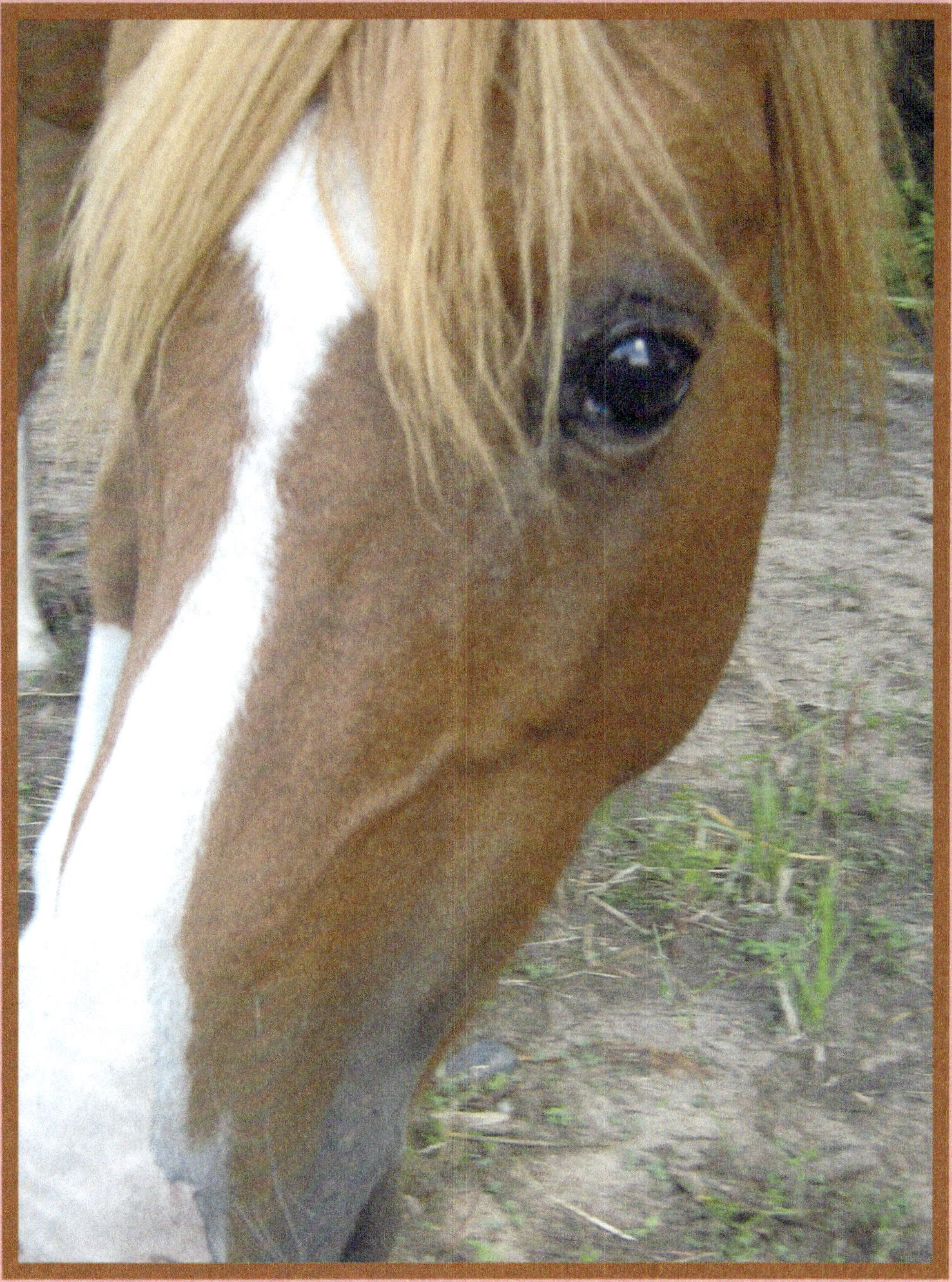

Weekly Planner-   Dates:

Monday

Tuesday

Wednesday

Thursday

Friday

Saturday

Sunday

To do

Notes

Notes, thoughts, ideas.

Weekly Planner- Dates:

Monday

Tuesday

Wednesday

Thursday

Friday

Saturday

Sunday

To do

Notes

Notes, thoughts, ideas.

Weekly Planner- Dates:

Monday

Tuesday

Wednesday

Thursday

Friday

Saturday

Sunday

To do

Notes

Notes, thoughts, ideas.

Weekly Planner- Dates:

Monday

Tuesday

Wednesday

Thursday

Friday

Saturday

Sunday

To do
-
-
-
-
-
-
-
-
-
-
-

Notes

Notes, thoughts, ideas.

Weekly Planner- Dates:

Monday

Tuesday

Wednesday

Thursday

Friday

Saturday

Sunday

To do

-
-
-
-
-
-
-
-
-

Notes

Notes, thoughts, ideas.

Weekly Planner- Dates:

Monday

Tuesday

Wednesday

Thursday

Friday

Satuday

Sunday

To do

-
-
-
-
-
-
-
-
-
-
-
-

Notes

Notes, thoughts, ideas.

Weekly Planner- Dates:

Monday

Tuesday

Wednesday

Thursday

Friday

Saturday

Sunday

To do
-
-
-
-
-
-
-
-
-
-

Notes

Notes, thoughts, ideas.

Weekly Planner- Dates:

Monday

Tuesday

Wednesday

Thursday

Friday

Saturday

Sunday

To do

Notes

Notes, thoughts, ideas.

Weekly Planner- Dates:

Monday

Tuesday

Wednesday

Thursday

Friday

Saturday

Sunday

To do
-
-
-
-
-
-
-
-
-
-

Notes

Notes, thoughts, ideas.

Weekly Planner- Dates:

Monday

Tuesday

Wednesday

Thursday

Friday

Saturday

Sunday

To do
-
-
-
-
-
-
-
-
-
-
-

Notes

Notes, thoughts, ideas.

Weekly Planner- Dates:

Monday

Tuesday

Wednesday

Thursday

Friday

Saturday

Sunday

To do

Notes

Notes, thoughts, ideas.